THE ULTIMATE

10

Sports

CLASSIC RIVALRIES

By Mark Stewart

Gareth Stevens
Publishing

Please visit our web site at www.garethstevens.com.
For a free catalog describing Gareth Stevens Publishing's list of high-quality books, call 1-800-542-2595 (USA) or 1-800-387-3178 (Canada). Gareth Stevens Publishing's fax: 1-877-542-2596

Library of Congress Cataloging-in-Publication Data available upon request from the publisher.
ISBN-10: 0-8368-9161-9 (lib. bdg.)
ISBN-13: 978-0-8368-9161-4 (lib. bdg.)

This edition first published in 2009 by
Gareth Stevens Publishing
A Weekly Reader® Company
1 Reader's Digest Road
Pleasantville, NY 10570-7000 USA

Copyright © 2009 by Gareth Stevens, Inc.

Executive Managing Editor: Lisa M. Herrington
Senior Editor: Brian Fitzgerald
Creative Director: Lisa Donovan
Senior Designer: Keith Plechaty
Photo Researcher: Charlene Pinckney
Publisher: Keith Garton

Picture credits
Key: t = top, b = bottom
Cover, title page: Jesse D. Garrabrant/NBAE/Getty Images; pp.4–5: Kevin C. Cox/Getty Images; p. 7: Winslow Townson/ AP Images; p. 8: (t) Dick Druckman/AP Images, (b) Bettmann/Corbis; p. 9: Doug Pensinger/Getty Images; p. 11: Streeter Lecka/Getty Images; p. 12: (t) Bob Donnan/US Presswire, (b) Malcolm Emmons/US Presswire; p. 13: Craig Jones/ Getty Images; p. 15: Joe Robbins/US Presswire; p. 16: (t) Duane Burleson/Ap Images, (b) Doug Sheridan/AP Images; p. 17: Matthew Emmons/Us Presswire; p. 19: Kevork Djansezian/AP Images; p. 20: (t) Focus on Sport/Getty Images, (b) Andrew D. Bernstein/NBAE via Getty Images; p. 21 Bettmann/Corbis; p. 23: Tim Heitman/US Presswire; p. 24: (t) Russ Russell/Getty Images, (b) Malcolm Emmons/US Presswire; p. 25: Nate Fine/Getty Images; p. 27: Robert H. Houston/ AP Images; p. 28: (t) AP Images, (b) Malcolm Emmons/US Presswire; p. 29: Bernstein Associates/Getty Images; p. 31: AP Images; p. 32: (t) Bettmann/Corbis; p. 33: Mitsunori Chigita/AP Images; p. 35: J. Meric/Getty Images; p. 36: (t) AP Images, (b) US Presswire; p. 37: Steve Coleman/AP Images; p. 39: Bob Child/AP Images; p. 40: (both) Elsa/Getty Images; p. 41: John Dunn/Icon SMI/Corbis; p. 43: Brian Spurlock/US Presswire; p. 44: (t) Terry Renna/AP Images, (b) George Tiedemann/Zuma Press; p. 45: Phil Coale/AP Images; p. 46: (t) Reuters/Corbis, (b) Adam Stoltzman/AP Images.

Printed in the United States of America

1 2 3 4 5 6 7 8 9 10 09 08

Cover: Paul Pierce of the Boston Celtics attempts a shot against the Los Angeles Lakers. The two teams met in the 2008 NBA Finals. Their rivalry dates back to the 1950s.

TABLE OF CONTENTS

Words in the glossary appear in **bold** type
the first time they are used in the text.

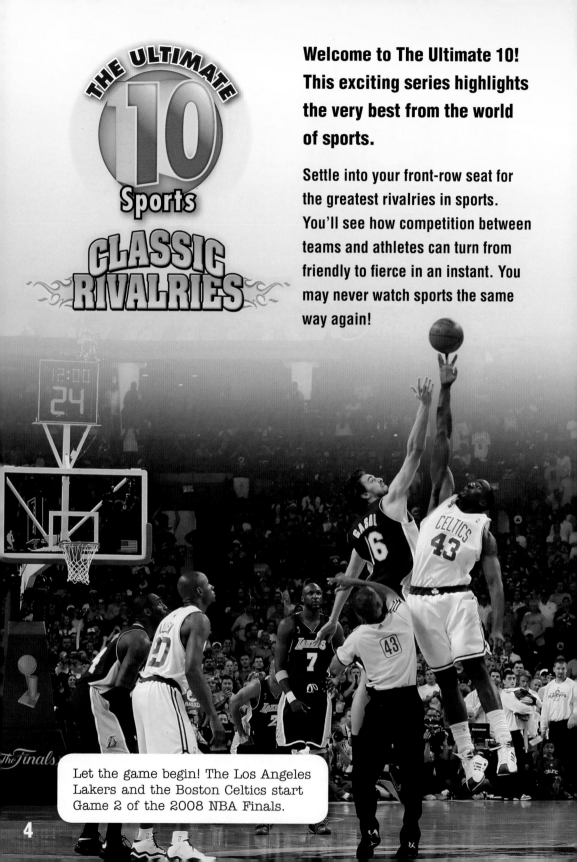

THE ULTIMATE 10 Sports

CLASSIC RIVALRIES

Welcome to The Ultimate 10! This exciting series highlights the very best from the world of sports.

Settle into your front-row seat for the greatest rivalries in sports. You'll see how competition between teams and athletes can turn from friendly to fierce in an instant. You may never watch sports the same way again!

Let the game begin! The Los Angeles Lakers and the Boston Celtics start Game 2 of the 2008 NBA Finals.

What makes a great sports rivalry? It starts when winning and losing become "personal." Sometimes athletes and fans can't remember exactly how a rivalry started. They just know that they *have to* beat their biggest rival.

This book tells the stories of 10 "ultimate" rivalries. These battles take place between cities, colleges, and individual athletes. Some rivalries are new and some are old, but they all have one thing in common. On game day, there is nothing else a true sports fan would rather be watching.

Famous Feuds

Here are 10 of the most heated rivalries in sports.

#1 Boston Red Sox vs. New York Yankees

#2 Duke Blue Devils vs. North Carolina Tar Heels

#3 Ohio State Buckeyes vs. Michigan Wolverines

#4 Boston Celtics vs. Los Angeles Lakers

#5 Dallas Cowboys vs. Washington Redskins

#6 Los Angeles Dodgers vs. San Francisco Giants

#7 Muhammad Ali vs. Joe Frazier

#8 Florida Gators vs. Florida State Seminoles

#9 Connecticut Huskies vs. Tennessee Lady Volunteers

#10 Dale Earnhardt vs. Jeff Gordon

#1

Boston Red Sox vs. New York Yankees

Teams from Boston and New York don't like each other. That's true in every professional sport. But no rivalry is bigger than the one between the Yankees and the Red Sox. The trouble began in 1920. That's when Boston sold its best player, Babe Ruth, to New York. A growing rivalry finally boiled over in the 1970s. No one has been able to turn down the heat ever since.

FAST FACTS

BOSTON RED SOX	NEW YORK YANKEES
HOME FIELD: Fenway Park	**HOME FIELD:** Yankee Stadium
FIRST WORLD SERIES CHAMPIONSHIP: 1903	**FIRST WORLD SERIES CHAMPIONSHIP:** 1923

An umpire separates Boston's Jason Varitek and New York's Alex Rodriguez. He knows the Red Sox–Yankees rivalry can explode at any moment.

Roots of the Rivalry

With Babe Ruth, the Red Sox were the best team in the American League. After Ruth joined the Yankees, the fortunes of both teams changed. The Yankees won 26 World Series over the next 80 years. They had stars such as Lou Gehrig, Joe DiMaggio, Yogi Berra, and Mickey Mantle.

"You've got to beat the Yankees. I've heard it about a thousand times."

—Red Sox manager Terry Francona

The Red Sox put some great players on the field, too. But they fell short of a championship year after year. Many Boston fans believed the team was "cursed" after selling Ruth to the Yankees. The Red Sox won **pennants** in 1946, 1967, 1975, and 1986. Each time, they lost the World Series in seven games.

Aaron Boone launches his pennant-winning home run in 2003.

Yankees Win!

The Yankees have always had star players. But the heroes of their biggest wins over Boston have been "little guys." In 1978, the teams played a one-game playoff in Boston. The Red Sox led 2–0 in the seventh inning. Light-hitting Bucky Dent hit a three-run homer to put the Yankees ahead for good.

In 2003, the teams met in the American League Championship Series (ALCS). The Red Sox were just five outs away from winning. The Yankees fought back to tie the score. The game went into extra innings. In the 11th inning, Aaron Boone clubbed a home run to send New York to the World Series.

HEAD TO HEAD

During the 1940s, New York and Boston fans had even more to argue about. Who was the best player in baseball? Was it New York's Joe DiMaggio or Boston's Ted Williams? In 1941, both players were at their best. Williams batted an incredible .406. DiMaggio had a record 56-game hitting streak. He beat out Williams for the Most Valuable Player (MVP) award.

Ted Williams and Joe DiMaggio pose together before a game.

Red Sox Win!

The Red Sox finally lifted the curse in 2004. They fell behind the Yankees three games to none in the ALCS. No baseball team had ever come back from that far behind in the playoffs. But Boston made history by winning the next four games. David Ortiz, Johnny Damon, and Curt Schilling led the amazing comeback. One week later, the Red Sox won the World Series.

A Look Ahead

Loyal fans fill up Yankee Stadium and Fenway Park for every game. That means the teams can afford to sign baseball's top players. Both clubs have also developed young stars in their minor leagues. The players may change, but the rivalry is sure to stay just as intense for years.

"Boston and New York are the ultimate places to play baseball."
—Yankees third baseman Alex Rodriguez

Johnny Damon watches his **grand slam** leave the ballpark in Game 7 of the 2004 ALCS. Two seasons later, Damon joined the Yankees!

DID YOU KNOW?

In 1901, the Red Sox and the Yankees played the first game in American League history. The Yankees were called the Baltimore Orioles at the time. The team moved to New York and became the Highlanders in 1903. The team was not called the Yankees until 1913.

#2

Duke Blue Devils vs. North Carolina Tar Heels

Basketball is king in North Carolina. Most years, the University of North Carolina (UNC) and Duke University compete for the college basketball title. The real prize for fans, however, is the right to say "we won" after the teams play. Students at the two colleges get along most of the year. But on game day, they become mortal enemies.

FAST FACTS

DUKE UNIVERSITY BLUE DEVILS	UNIVERSITY OF NORTH CAROLINA TAR HEELS
HOME COURT: Cameron Indoor Stadium	**HOME COURT:** Dean Smith Center
FIRST CONFERENCE CHAMPIONSHIP: 1960	**FIRST CONFERENCE CHAMPIONSHIP:** 1957

Duke's famous "Cameron Crazies" try to distract UNC's Danny Green during a 2008 game. The students are as much a part of the Duke–North Carolina rivalry as the players.

Roots of the Rivalry

Duke and UNC are less than a half-hour's drive apart. The schools had a "friendly" rivalry until the 1960s. That changed in 1961 when Duke's Art Heyman and Carolina's Larry Brown had a fight on the court. During the 1970s and 1980s, the rivalry continued to heat up.

Top of the Game

From 1988 to 1992, the rivalry was at its peak. The two schools met in the Atlantic Coast Conference (ACC) championship game four times. Each team won twice. In 1991 and 1992, the Blue Devils won the **NCAA Tournament**. In 1993, the Tar Heels were national champions.

> **Anybody who dreams of playing college basketball dreams of playing in this game.**
> —North Carolina forward Marcus Ginyard

HEAD TO HEAD

Great coaches make a great rivalry. During the 1980s and 1990s, Dean Smith and Mike Krzyzewski led their teams into battle. Both are coaching legends. UNC's Smith retired in 1997 with 879 career wins. Duke's "Coach K" won his 800th game in 2008. Roy Williams took over the Tar Heels in 2003. He led Carolina to the national championship in his second season.

Coach K gives some quick advice to sharpshooter J.J. Redick.

Tar Heels Win!

In 1984, Michael Jordan and Sam Perkins played their last home game for UNC. The number-one ranked Tar Heels trailed the Blue Devils late in the game. Duke missed **free throws** that would have sealed a win. UNC's Matt Doherty dribbled the length of the court and tied the score. His 15-foot jump shot barely beat the buzzer. The game was still tied after one **overtime**. In the second overtime, Jordan and Perkins were unstoppable. Carolina won 96–83.

Michael Jordan rises to the hoop against the Blue Devils.

Blue Devils Win!

In a 1998 game, freshman Elton Brand led Duke on an amazing comeback. The Blue Devils trailed the Tar Heels by 17 points with 12 minutes left. Duke came storming back to win 77–75. Brand also made a great comeback. Two months earlier, he had broken his foot. Many thought he would be out for the season. The victory was the 500th for Coach K. The win also gave Duke the ACC regular-season championship.

Elton Brand works his way toward the basket. Great players like Brand continue to fuel the rivalry.

A Look Ahead

Duke and Carolina have played dozens of times since 1960. In each of those games, at least one team has been ranked in the Top 25. That may never change. As long as there is a rivalry, the schools will continue drawing the nation's top basketball talent.

"There's more hate involved when it comes to the fans. When it comes to the players, there's a lot of respect."

—Duke guard J.J. Redick

DID YOU KNOW?

Great rivalries mean great players. Through 2008, the two schools had the NCAA Player of the Year 10 times. UNC stars Michael Jordan, Antawn Jamison, and Tyler Hansbrough have won the award. The award winners for Duke include Christian Laettner, Elton Brand, and J.J. Redick.

#3
Ohio State Buckeyes vs. Michigan Wolverines

The fiercest football rivalry of the 21st century began back in the 19th century. Michigan and Ohio State have been banging heads since 1897. Often the outcome decides the champion of the Big Ten Conference. Each year, the players seem to tackle and block a little bit harder than they did the season before. That's what happens when two schools have spent more than a 100 years playing for pride.

FAST FACTS

OHIO STATE UNIVERSITY BUCKEYES	UNIVERSITY OF MICHIGAN WOLVERINES
HOME FIELD: Ohio Stadium	**HOME FIELD:** Michigan Stadium
FIRST CONFERENCE CHAMPIONSHIP: 1916	**FIRST CONFERENCE CHAMPIONSHIP:** 1898

> "Legends are made in this game."
> —Ohio State lineman T.J. Downing

Michigan running back Mike Hart runs into a wall of Buckeyes during the 2006 game. It was the 103rd meeting between the teams.

Roots of the Rivalry

In the early 1900s, Michigan had the best team in the country. Ohio State finally beat Michigan in 1919. The rivalry reached a fever pitch in the 1930s. The Buckeyes won four games in a row without allowing a point. Since then, the rivalry has seesawed back and forth. Each year, the teams battle on the final day of the Big Ten season.

The Snow Bowl

The strangest game in the rivalry took place in 1950. The teams played in a blizzard. Michigan and Ohio State punted a combined 45 times—often on first down! The plan was to make the other team fumble on the icy field. Michigan did not make a first down but won the game 9–3. The Wolverines scored a touchdown and a **safety** on two blocked punts.

Wolverines Win!

In 1997, the Wolverines needed to beat the Buckeyes to keep their perfect season going. Defensive back Charles Woodson made sure they got it. He caught a long pass to set up Michigan's first touchdown. He scored on a 78-yard punt return for the second touchdown. He also intercepted a pass in the end zone. The Wolverines won 20–14. They went on to win the Rose Bowl and shared the NCAA championship with Nebraska. Woodson won the **Heisman Trophy** as the nation's top player.

The Buckeyes watch helplessly as Charles Woodson breezes to the end zone.

HEAD TO HEAD

The Wolverines and the Buckeyes players don't like each other very much. The biggest rivalry, however, was between two of their coaches. Bo Schembechler and Woody Hayes faced each other 10 times in the 1960s and 1970s. Schembechler's Wolverines won five of those games, lost four, and tied once. Michigan and Ohio State shared the conference title six times during those years. Fans still call it "the 10-Year War."

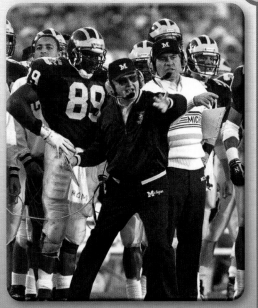

Bo Schembechler directs the Wolverines from the sidelines.

Buckeyes Win!

Before the 2006 game, Ohio State was ranked number 1 and Michigan was number 2. That had never happened before. Fans called it "the game of the century." Three touchdown passes by Troy Smith helped the Buckeyes to a 28–14 lead at halftime. But the Wolverines would not give up. Smith threw for another touchdown, and Ohio State held on to win 42–39. Smith was later awarded the Heisman Trophy.

Troy Smith scans the field with a Michigan pass rusher in hot pursuit.

A Look Ahead

This rivalry stays hot even when one of the teams is not. In recent years, Ohio State has battled for the national championship. Michigan, however, was not a top team. Even so, Ohio State–Michigan was still the game of the year for both teams. That may never change.

> **"If you aren't on your deathbed, you will be playing in that game."**
>
> —Michigan lineman Eric Wilson

DID YOU KNOW?

In 2003, Ohio State and Michigan met for the 100th time. The game set a record for the biggest crowd ever at a college game. More than 112,000 fans packed into Michigan Stadium, known as "the Big House." Running back Chris Perry and receiver Braylon Edwards led the Wolverines to a 35–21 win.

Boston Celtics vs. Los Angeles Lakers

The National Basketball Association (NBA) held 62 championship series from 1947 to 2008. The Lakers and the Celtics won exactly half of them. No other sport has two teams that have been so good for so long. No other NBA teams can claim a greater collection of stars. Basketball is a contest of speed, strength, and skill. When Los Angeles and Boston play, it's a war.

FAST FACTS

BOSTON CELTICS	LOS ANGELES LAKERS
HOME COURT: TD Banknorth Garden	**HOME COURT:** The Staples Center
FIRST NBA CHAMPIONSHIP: 1957	**FIRST NBA CHAMPIONSHIP:** 1949

Roots of the Rivalry

The two teams first met in the NBA Finals in 1959. At the time, the Lakers called Minneapolis home. The rivalry turned into an East Coast–West Coast battle after the team moved to Los Angeles in 1960.

The Lakers often had the better individual players, including Elgin Baylor and Jerry West. The Celtics, however, had the better team. Led by coach Red Auerbach, Boston played unselfish basketball. Stars such as Bill Russell and Bob Cousy played great together. The Celtics met the Lakers for the championship seven times from 1959 to 1969. Boston's "team first" style won out every time.

Kobe Bryant challenges Kevin Garnett during the 2008 NBA Finals. For Lakers and Celtics fans, it was just like old times!

❝ What they had back then was something that was truly magical. ❞
—Lakers guard Kobe Bryant, on the early days of the Celtics–Lakers rivalry

19

Jerry West tries a layup against Bill Russell during the 1969 NBA Finals. The Lakers lost, but the high-scoring West was named Finals MVP.

Celtics Win!

By the end of the 1960s, the Celtics stars were getting old. As the Lakers discovered, Boston could never be counted out. In the 1969 NBA Finals, Jerry West, Elgin Baylor, and Wilt Chamberlain seemed to have Boston beaten. But the Celtics pushed the series to Game 7. In the final minutes, West and Chamberlain were slowed by injuries. The Celtics won 108–106. Their win ruined L.A.'s plans for a victory celebration. The team had hung thousands of balloons in large nets over the court. That's where they stayed!

HEAD TO HEAD

In the 1980s, Magic Johnson and Larry Bird took the rivalry to a new level. Magic's Lakers played a flashy style of basketball called "Showtime." Bird's Celtics were tough and made the most of their talent. Both players had the drive to win at any cost. Magic and Bird met in the Finals three times. Their matchups made the NBA more popular than ever before.

Larry Bird and Magic Johnson fight for position near the basket.

Lakers Win!

In 1984, Larry Bird and Boston beat the Lakers in a thrilling championship series. One year later, the teams met again. In Game 1, the Celtics crushed the Lakers 148–114. Los Angeles recovered and won four of the next five games. James Worthy, Magic Johnson, and Kareem Abdul-Jabbar starred on offense. Michael Cooper's tough defense kept Larry Bird off his game. For the first time, L.A. had beaten Boston in the Finals!

A Look Ahead

The 2008 NBA Finals were just like old times. Kobe Bryant led L.A. against Boston's Paul Pierce, Kevin Garnett, and Ray Allen. Just as they had in the 1960s, the Celtics won out. For thrills and chills, no other rivalry in pro basketball comes close.

Boston's Robert Parish and Kevin McHale try to stop Kareem Abdul-Jabbar during the 1985 NBA Finals.

❝I geared everything to playing the Finals against the Lakers.❞
—Celtics star Larry Bird

DID YOU KNOW?

Starting in 1957, the Celtics won the NBA championship 11 times in 13 seasons. Their 2008 win was their 17th championship. The Lakers have been league champions 14 times.

#5

Dallas Cowboys vs. Washington Redskins

The Washington Redskins represent the nation's capital. The popular Dallas Cowboys are called "America's Team." Since 1961, the teams have played twice a year. From the opening kickoff, millions of Americans stop what they are doing. For true fans, nothing compares with watching the best rivalry in the National Football League (NFL).

FAST FACTS

DALLAS COWBOYS	WASHINGTON REDSKINS
HOME FIELD: Texas Stadium	**HOME FIELD:** FedEx Field
FIRST CHAMPIONSHIP: 1971	**FIRST CHAMPIONSHIP:** 1937

Washington's Clinton Portis takes on two Dallas players in 2008. Both teams seem to block and tackle a little bit harder whenever they meet.

Roots of the Rivalry

In 1958, a Texas millionaire named Clint Murchison made a deal to buy the Redskins. He wanted to move the team to Dallas. Washington's owner backed out at the last minute. Murchison was furious. He started a new NFL team, the Cowboys, two years later. The Redskins and the Cowboys have been bitter enemies ever since.

A Matter of Pride

The Cowboys and the Redskins play in the Eastern Division of the National Football Conference (NFC). The teams often battle for the division championship. Even when the games are not important in the **standings**, they are special for fans and players. Past stars still talk about the Cowboys–Redskins games as if they were the only ones that mattered.

Clint Longley fires a long pass against Washington in 1974. Fans called him "the Mad Bomber" after that game.

Cowboys Win!

The star of Dallas's most famous victory was a little-known player. On Thanksgiving Day in 1974, the Redskins knocked Dallas quarterback Roger Staubach out of the game. **Rookie** Clint Longley took his place. Longley threw a 50-yard touchdown pass in the final seconds to win 24–23. Longley is still a hero in Dallas. Redskins coach George Allen said the loss was probably the toughest his team ever had.

HEAD TO HEAD

A great football rivalry begins with the quarterbacks. Some of the best were Dallas's Roger Staubach and Troy Aikman and Washington's Billy Kilmer and Joe Theismann. The best quarterback duels? They were between Sonny Jurgensen of Washington and Don Meredith of Dallas. In four games from 1965 to 1967, their teams combined for 222 points. Each game was decided by three points or less.

Don Meredith escapes the pass rush during a 1967 game against Washington.

Redskins Win!

Washington and Dallas were already fierce rivals by 1972. The rivalry went up a notch when the teams met in the NFC Championship Game. The winner would go to the Super Bowl. The loser would go home. Billy Kilmer threw two touchdown passes to Charley Taylor. The Washington defense held Dallas to just a field goal. The Redskins won 26–3.

Charley Taylor reaches the end zone with a Dallas defender on his back.

A Look Ahead

Nothing can stop a great football rivalry. Fans of the Cowboys and the Redskins know that better than anyone. The players, the coaches, and even the stadiums have changed. New stars such as Tony Romo and Jason Campbell have joined the feud. But when Dallas and Washington take the field, it is always good old-fashioned football at its best.

> **"We don't like them, they don't like us."**
> —Cowboys quarterback
> Roger Staubach

DID YOU KNOW?

In their first season, 1960, the Cowboys were the worst team in the NFL. They didn't win a single game. The Redskins were not much better. Their only win that season came against—who else?—the Cowboys!

Los Angeles Dodgers vs. San Francisco Giants

From 1890 to 1957, the Dodgers played in Brooklyn, New York. The Giants played a few miles away, in Manhattan. They competed for the National League pennant every year. In 1958, both teams headed to California. The change of addresses turned a citywide rivalry into a statewide rivalry. It also brought in millions of new fans. After more than 120 years, the rivalry is as fierce as ever.

FAST FACTS

LOS ANGELES DODGERS	SAN FRANCISCO GIANTS
HOME FIELD: Dodger Stadium	**HOME FIELD:** AT&T Park
FIRST CHAMPIONSHIP: 1890	**FIRST CHAMPIONSHIP:** 1888

The Giants–Dodgers rivalry explodes in 1965. San Francisco's Juan Marichal wrestles with catcher Johnny Roseboro. Dodgers pitcher Sandy Koufax rushes in to break up the fight.

Roots of the Rivalry

During their days in New York, the Giants and the Dodgers hated each other. The players got into fights on the field and off. So did the fans. When the Dodgers traded Jackie Robinson to the Giants, he could not bear the thought of switching uniforms. Instead, he quit baseball!

The Wild West

The rivalry reached a fever pitch after the teams moved to California. San Francisco's powerful lineup included stars Willie Mays and Willie McCovey. Sandy Koufax led a great Dodgers pitching staff. In 1962, the two teams finished in a tie. The season came down to the last game of a three-game playoff. The Giants scored four runs in the ninth inning to win the pennant.

> **" The Giants–Dodgers rivalry lives on. It's the way it used to be for so many years and the way it is now. "**
>
> —Dodgers manager
> Tommy Lasorda

Bobby Thomson watches his famous home run. That one swing broke the hearts of Dodgers fans.

Giants Win!

In 1951, the Dodgers and the Giants finished the season tied for first place. A three-game playoff would decide which team would go to the World Series. The teams split the first two games. In Game 3, the Dodgers led 4–1 in the bottom of the ninth inning. Brooklyn pitcher Don Newcombe gave up a run and put two runners on base. The Dodgers brought in Ralph Branca to close out the game. He gave up a home run to Bobby Thomson that won the pennant for the Giants. That legendary homer is known as "the Shot Heard 'Round the World."

HEAD TO HEAD

The Dodgers–Giants rivalry was at its best when Sandy Koufax and Juan Marichal took the mound. They were the two best pitchers in the National League. In 1963, Koufax pitched a no-hitter against the Giants. That same year, Marichal tied Koufax for the league lead with 25 wins. From 1963 to 1966, each pitcher averaged more than 23 wins a season. Both were later elected to the **Hall of Fame**.

Sandy Koufax fires a fastball. He once struck out 18 Giants in a game.

Dodgers Win!

Nothing is better than winning a pennant. In this rivalry, however, keeping the other team from winning is almost as good. The teams met on the last day of the 1993 season. The Giants had won an amazing 103 games. Still, they needed one more win to reach the playoffs. Mike Piazza, a rookie catcher for the Dodgers, belted two home runs. The Dodgers crushed the Giants 12–1 to keep them out of the playoffs.

A Look Ahead

After more than 2,000 games, the Dodgers and the Giants are almost dead even. When these two teams play, win-loss records don't matter. There will always be something much bigger at stake.

Mike Piazza gets high fives from a teammate after hitting one of his two homers against the Giants.

The Giants' main rivals were not always called the Dodgers. In its early years, the Brooklyn team had a number of different names. They included the Bridegrooms, the Superbas, and the Robins. The team has been known as the Dodgers since 1931.

#7
Muhammad Ali vs.
Joe Frazier

Muhammad Ali and Joe Frazier could not have been more different. Their styles were like night and day. Ali used his great footwork and fast hands to beat opponents. Frazier punished other boxers with his powerful punches. In the 1970s, Ali and Frazier fought three legendary matches. Fans everywhere took sides. It was impossible not to root for one of these two champions once the opening bell rang.

FAST FACTS

MUHAMMAD ALI	JOE FRAZIER
PRO RECORD:	**PRO RECORD:**
56–5–0 (37 Knockouts)	32–4–1 (27 Knockouts)
HEAVYWEIGHT CHAMPION:	**HEAVYWEIGHT CHAMPION:**
1964 to 1967, 1974 to 1978, 1978 to 1979	1968 to 1973

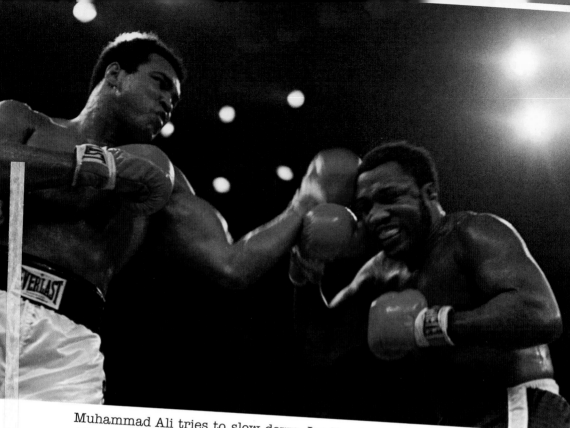

Muhammad Ali tries to slow down Joe Frazier with a left jab. Ali was taller and quicker, but Frazier never stopped attacking.

Roots of the Rivalry

In 1967, Muhammad Ali was the best boxer in the world. He was heavyweight champion and had won 29 straight fights. Ali was stripped of his title, however. He had been drafted into the Army but refused to join because of religious reasons. Unable to box, Ali traveled the country giving speeches. He told young people to stand up for their beliefs, no matter what the cost—just as he had.

> **❝Joe Frazier is so ugly that when he cries, the tears turn around and go down the back of his head.❞**
>
> —Muhammad Ali

During Ali's time away from boxing, Joe Frazier became **heavyweight** champion. No one could remember a tougher boxer. Ali was allowed to fight again in 1970. Fans could hardly wait for the first Ali–Frazier **bout**.

Joe Frazier and Muhammad Ali have a war of words before their first meeting in the ring.

Frazier Wins!

Frazier's advisers told him not to fight Ali. Ali convinced Frazier that he would not be a true champion until he did. Frazier agreed to fight Ali in 1971. When they met in the ring, Ali was still not in top shape. By the final round, he was exhausted. Frazier knocked him to the canvas, but Ali got up before the count of 10. In the end, the judges gave the **decision** to Frazier.

HEAD TO HEAD

Ali and Frazier were very different fighters. Ali moved quickly from side to side. He threw lightning-quick jabs. Frazier was always on the attack. He was not afraid to get hit two or three times to land one big punch of his own. Here is how the two fighters matched up.

FIGHTER	CATEGORY	FIGHTER
MUHAMMAD ALI		JOE FRAZIER
January 17, 1942	Birth Date	January 12, 1944
6 feet 3 inches	Height	5 feet 11½ inches
210½ pounds	Weight	205 pounds
82 inches	Reach	73½ inches

Ali Wins!

Ali and Frazier fought again in 1974. It was a non-title fight. Frazier had lost the championship to George Foreman. Ali defeated Frazier in a 12-round decision. Later that year, Ali knocked out Foreman to win the heavyweight title for a second time.

> **"I hit him with punches that would bring down the walls of a city, and he still kept coming."**
> —Joe Frazier, after the Thrilla in Manila

The third and final bout took place in Manila in the Philippines. "The Thrilla in Manila" is considered one of the greatest fights of all time. Both boxers dished out and received heavy punishment. Frazier failed to answer the bell for the 15th round. Ali barely celebrated. He was too exhausted.

The two champions slug it out during the Thrilla in Manila.

DID YOU KNOW?

Neither fighter was the same after their third bout. Ali no longer had his great speed. He lost his title to Leon Spinks in 1978. Frazier retired after two more fights. Ali retired after losing to Trevor Berbick in 1981.

#8

Florida Gators vs. Florida State Seminoles

Warm fall afternoons get sizzling-hot when the University of Florida and Florida State play. For more than 50 years, the Gators and the Seminoles have competed for the state's best young players—and then sent them into battle on the field. In most of Florida, you are either a Gators fan or a Seminoles fan. On game day, there is no middle ground.

FAST FACTS

UNIVERSITY OF FLORIDA GATORS	FLORIDA STATE UNIVERSITY SEMINOLES
HOME FIELD: Ben Hill Griffin Stadium	**HOME FIELD:** Doak Campbell Stadium
FIRST NATIONAL CHAMPIONSHIP: 1996	**FIRST NATIONAL CHAMPIONSHIP:** 1993

The Seminoles try to bring down Tim Tebow during the 2007 game. The Gators quarterback has been one of the biggest stars in the long rivalry.

Roots of the Rivalry

The University of Florida had a head start on Florida State in football. The Gators began playing more than 100 years ago. The Seminoles did not form a team until the late 1940s. The Gators and the Seminoles played their first game in 1958. The Gators beat the Seminoles 21–7. Back then, Florida had a more powerful team. The Gators won all but three of the first 19 games between the schools.

> **"It's not just a big game, it's everything to us."**
> —Florida State running back Warrick Dunn, on the yearly game against Florida

Things began to change when Florida State hired Bobby Bowden in 1976. Beginning in 1977, he led the Seminoles to four wins in a row. In 1990, the Gators hired coach Steve Spurrier. The rivalry went to a whole new level.

HEAD TO HEAD

During the 1990s, Bobby Bowden and Steve Spurrier matched wits 12 times. Their teams played 10 times in the regular season and twice in **bowl games**. Florida State had the edge with a 7-4-1 record. Bowden's Seminoles won two national titles during the 1990s. Spurrier's Gators won one.

The Seminoles carry Bobby Bowden off the field. They are celebrating his first win over Florida, in 1977.

Charlie Ward spots an open receiver during the 1993 game against Florida.

Seminoles Win!

In the 1993 game, fans saw two future Heisman Trophy winners do battle. Quarterback Charlie Ward led the Seminoles against Danny Wuerffel's Gators. The Florida State defense was sensational. It held the Gators to minus 33 rushing yards. Meanwhile, Ward threw for 446 yards and four touchdowns. He nailed down a 33–21 victory with a 79-yard pass to Warrick Dunn late in the fourth quarter. Ward later guided Florida State to the national championship.

Gators Win!

In 1996, the Gators lost to the Seminoles during the regular season, 24–21. They met again in January in the Sugar Bowl. This time, Florida was ready. Quarterback Danny Wuerffel threw three touchdown passes to Ike Hilliard. Wuerffel also ran for a score. The Gators blew out the Seminoles 52–20. The victory gave Florida its first-ever national championship.

Danny Wuerffel fires a pass against the Seminoles in the Sugar Bowl.

A Look Ahead

Every year, the state of Florida produces terrific high school players. The Gators and the Seminoles fight to **recruit** the top talent. As long as both schools get their fair share of young stars, the rivalry will only get better.

> **❝ We know at Florida that you can't win a national championship without going through Florida State. ❞**
>
> —former Florida coach Steve Spurrier

DID YOU KNOW?

In a heated rivalry, the smallest edge can make a big difference. In the 1960s, Florida coach Ray Graves wanted to keep the Gators from tiring on hot days. He asked scientists at his school for help. They invented a sports drink that became known as Gatorade!

#9

Connecticut Huskies vs. Tennessee Lady Volunteers

For years, the world of women's college hoops came down to two words: Tennessee and Connecticut. From 1995 to 2004, the schools won eight national championships. In seven of those eight seasons, they clashed in NCAA Tournament play. Will there ever be a better rivalry in women's sports? It's hard to say—this one's not over yet!

FAST FACTS

UNIVERSITY OF CONNECTICUT HUSKIES	UNIVERSITY OF TENNESSEE LADY VOLUNTEERS
HOME COURT: Gampel Pavilion	**HOME COURT:** Thompson-Boling Arena
FIRST NATIONAL CHAMPIONSHIP: 1995	**FIRST NATIONAL CHAMPIONSHIP:** 1987

Roots of the Rivalry

For years, the Tennessee Lady Volunteers were the team to beat in women's basketball. That was still true in 1995, when the University of Connecticut, or UConn, became a powerhouse. The Huskies were led by Rebecca Lobo, the college player of the year. UConn defeated Tennessee 77–64 in a January game and again in the national championship game.

Three in a Row

The rivalry heated up over the next few seasons. Tennessee won the next three NCAA Tournaments. In 1996 and 1997, the Lady Vols had to beat UConn to do it. Tennessee's star player was Chamique Holdsclaw. She was named player of the year after the 1998 championship.

Rebecca Lobo grabs a rebound during a win over Tennessee in 1995. She helped UConn become the top team that year.

"It's the greatest rivalry we have in our game. It's the clash of the giants."
—Tennessee guard Kara Lawson

Huskies Wins!

The Huskies rebuilt with great new players. By 2000, they were ready to recapture the NCAA title. Shea Ralph led UConn to a 71–52 victory over Tennessee in the championship game. During one stretch, UConn beat Tennessee six times in a row. That included wins over the Lady Volunteers in the championship game in 2003 and 2004. High-scoring guard Diana Taurasi was named Most Outstanding Player of the **Final Four** both years.

Diana Taurasi drives to the basket against Tennessee. She led UConn to two national championships.

HEAD TO HEAD

The games between Tennessee and Connecticut often come down to a battle of brains. Pat Summitt of the Lady Volunteers and Geno Auriemma of the Huskies are two of the best coaches in basketball. They have spent years trying to outsmart each other—both on and off the court. They often compete for the same high school stars. That only feeds the red-hot rivalry.

Pat Summitt and Geno Auriemma shake hands before the 2004 championship game.

Lady Vols Win!

Like all great teams, the Lady Volunteers learned from their losses. In 2007 and 2008, they reclaimed the national title. Tennessee's leader, Candace Parker, was the latest star in the rivalry. In her last game against the Huskies, she scored 30 points in 70–64 win. During the game, Parker raised the rivalry to new heights when she dunked the ball.

A Look Ahead

For 13 seasons, Tennessee and UConn met during the regular season. In 2007, the schools decided to stop playing their annual game. But that makes the rivalry even more special. The schools will meet only in the NCAA Tournament— where one team goes forward and the other goes home!

Candace Parker rises to the rim against UConn in 2007.

DID YOU KNOW?

In 2004, both the UConn men's and women's basketball teams won the national championship. That had never happened before in college basketball.

#10

Dale Earnhardt vs. Jeff Gordon

Dale Earnhardt was a tough, ornery "good old boy." He drove hard and he drove fast. Jeff Gordon was young, handsome, and friendly. He knew the right thing to do and say in any situation. Their rivalry was more than just a race to the finish line. It was a battle for the heart and soul of stock-car racing.

FAST FACTS

DALE EARNHARDT	JEFF GORDON
CAR NUMBER: 3	CAR NUMBER: 24
FIRST NASCAR CHAMPIONSHIP: 1980	FIRST NASCAR CHAMPIONSHIP: 1995

Jeff Gordon passes Dale Earnhardt during a 1996 race. The popularity of the two drivers created a red-hot rivalry between their fans, too.

Roots of the Rivalry

In the 1990s, **NASCAR** officials were trying to win new fans with a "cleaner" image. For years, stock-car racing was a sport linked to alcohol and tobacco. It also had an "outlaw" feel that some people thought was holding the sport back.

> **"**He plays video games, I go big-game hunting. He wears athletic shoes, I wear boots.**"**
>
> —Dale Earnhardt, on Jeff Gordon

Jeff Gordon was the new kind of driver NASCAR wanted. He was clean-cut and well mannered. When Gordon started winning races, NASCAR made him a star. That made Dale Earnhardt's fans angry. Earnhardt was "old school." He didn't mind getting dirty—or driving dirty, if that's what it took to win. Earnhardt's nickname said it all: He was "the Intimidator."

Gordon Wins!

The Daytona 500 is NASCAR's biggest race. It was also the one race that Earnhardt could not seem to win. In 1997, he was in the lead with 10 laps to go. Suddenly, he nicked the wall and swerved into Gordon's car. Gordon stayed in control. Two other cars hit Earnhardt from behind. His car ended up upside down on the track. Earnhardt watched in frustration as Gordon took the checkered flag for *his* first Daytona 500 victory.

Jeff Gordon gets a victory shower after winning the 1997 Daytona 500.

HEAD TO HEAD

Dale Earnhardt and Jeff Gordon could not have been more different off the track. On the track, they had one big thing in common: They won a lot of races. Here is how their careers look side by side.

	YEARS	WINS	NASCAR CHAMPIONSHIPS
JEFF GORDON*	1992–2008	81	4
DALE EARNHARDT	1975–2001	76	7

*Through 2008

Earnhardt Wins!

In 1998, Earnhardt started his 21st Daytona 500. His fans were beginning to think he would never win. But this time he did. He passed Gordon and roared into first place with 77 laps to go and held on to win. To show their respect, all of the **pit crews** hopped over the wall and lined the track as Earnhardt drove by.

Dale Earnhardt grabs the lead from Jeff Gordon on his way to victory in the 1998 Daytona 500.

End of an Era

Dale Earnhardt was killed in a crash at the 2001 Daytona 500. After his death, his fans hoped that his son Dale Jr. would continue the rivalry with Gordon. Dale Jr. won Daytona in 2004, and Gordon won it in 2005. But no one could replace the Intimidator.

> **"We loved to beat one another. We battled hard on the track, and he certainly didn't mind shoving me around."**
>
> —Jeff Gordon

DID YOU KNOW?

Jeff Gordon's first NASCAR race was also the last race for racing legend Richard Petty. Like Earnhardt, Petty was one of the sport's "old school" drivers. Both Petty and Earnhardt were seven-time NASCAR champions.

Honorable Mentions

Army vs. Navy
First Meeting: 1890

The U.S. Military Academy and the U.S. Naval Academy have been meeting on the football field for more than 100 years. Fans call the rivalry "the Civil War." After the players graduate, they don't go on to the pros. Instead, they become officers in the military. So when the teams meet on the field, they are truly playing for pride. Even in wartime, everyone in the Army and the Navy stops to see who wins the big game.

Chris Evert vs. Martina Navratilova
First Meeting: 1973

Today, women's tennis is as popular as men's tennis. Chris Evert and Martina Navratilova had a lot to do with that. During the 1970s and 1980s, they changed the way tennis was played. Evert's mistake-free style forced Navratilova to sharpen her game. Navratilova's incredible fitness forced Evert to get serious about her own training. As these rivals got better, they pulled all of women's tennis into the modern age.

Glossary

bout: a boxing match

bowl games: games played after the regular season by the top college football teams

decision: a victory decided by boxing judges when a fight does not end in a knockout

Final Four: the championship round of the NCAA Tournament. The last four teams in the tournament play two semifinal games. The winners advance to the championship game.

free throws: shots awarded to a player after a foul. Each made free throw, or foul shot, is worth one point.

grand slam: a home run with the bases loaded (runners on first, second, and third bases)

Hall of Fame: a museum that honors the greatest athletes in a sport

heavyweight: a division for boxers who weigh more than 200 pounds (91 kilograms)

Heisman Trophy: an award that honors the best player in college football each season

NASCAR: the National Association for Stock Car Auto Racing. A stock car is shaped like a car found "in stock" at an auto dealership.

NCAA Tournament: a competition to decide the champion of college basketball. *NCAA* stands for *National Collegiate Athletic Association.*

overtime: an extra period played when a game is tied at the end of regular time

pennants: league championships. The pennant winners of the American League and the National League meet in the World Series.

pit crews: members of racing teams who work on cars during refueling stops

recruit: to try to convince high school athletes to attend a college

rookie: a player in his or her first season as a professional

safety: a two-point score by the defense in football. A team may score a safety in several ways, most often when a defensive player tackles a ball carrier in his own end zone.

standings: a list of teams and their playing records, starting with the best and ending with the worst

For More Information

Books

Buckley, Jim and David Fischer. *Greatest Sports Rivalries.* New York: Barnes & Noble, 2005.

Dortch, Chris. *Greatest Rivalries in Sports.* New York: Sports Illustrated for Kids, 2005.

Web Sites

Major League Baseball
mlb.com

The National Basketball Association
www.nba.com

The National Football League
www.nfl.com

Index

About the Author

Mark Stewart is the "ultimate" sports author. He has written more than 100 books on the top teams and athletes in college and the pros. Mark has met many of the people who fueled the rivalries in this book, including Muhammad Ali, Juan Marichal, Mike Krzyzewski, Rebecca Lobo, and Martina Navratilova. In 1996, he worked with Jeff Gordon on the driver's first authorized biography.